A Place That Cares . . .

"When you're young and looking for your first job you can't help but wonder where you're meant to go and what you're meant to do. When I told my friends that I'd be working at a cancer center most of them were skeptical, and I have to admit that, standing outside of the antiquated red building on a bitterly cold January day, I began to doubt the sanity of this decision myself. I didn't know then that there was a lot to be learned inside those walls, important things like love, and care, and, above all else, faith. Those same walls were to hold many surprises, a lot of laughter; and a quality of living I'd never have thought possible. . . ."

Please Remember Me

A Young Woman's Story
of Her Friendship with an
Unforgettable
Fifteen-Year-Old Boy.

Mari Brady

AN ARCHWAY PAPERBACK
POCKET BOOKS • NEW YORK

Acknowledgment

On behalf of the Banks family and myself I would like to acknowledge Graham's three doctors and their teams for the time, care, and compassion that they gave to him: Edward J. Beattie, Jr., M.D., Robert B. Golbey, M.D., Willet F. Whitmore, Jr., M.D.

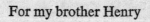

For my brother Henry

"When it's time to die let us not discover that we never lived"

Thoreau

Chapter One

When you're young and looking for your first job you can't help but wonder where you're meant to go and what you're meant to do. When I told my friends that I'd be working at a cancer center most of them were skeptical, and I have to admit that, standing outside of the antiquated red brick building on a bitterly cold January day, I began to doubt the sanity of this decision myself. I didn't know then that there was a lot to be learned inside those walls, important things like love, and care, and, above all else, faith. Those same walls were to hold many surprises, a lot of laughter, and a quality of living I'd never have thought possible.

Eight months later, on a September morning, as I balanced one Monopoly game, a chess and checkers set, the materials for a decoupage project, four decks of cards, and, last but not least, the current issue of *Playboy* magazine in my arms, I thought, this was one aspect of the job they neglected to tell us about. I checked my list and, seeing that I had everything, hung our tacky "Be Back Soon" sign on the door and started off down the second-floor corridor toward Ewing 5.

No, there wasn't a word anywhere about pushing pianos, lugging heavy baskets of bottles, climbing in and out of crates for assorted decorations, or baby-sitting for infants and dogs "in our spare time." In fact, when I applied for the job of recreation worker it was for Memorial Sloan-Kettering, not realizing at the time that Ewing, which had been a city hospital, was even a part of the complex. I continued down the hallway that led to the X-ray Department in the Outpatient Building, and down yet another corridor past Radiation Therapy to the self-service elevator at the end. I remembered the first time I ever made this trip. The directions were sketchy at best: "Just follow the yellow line," the nurse said, "you can't possibly get lost." Well, she was wrong—I could and I did. The yellow line somehow eluded me and before I knew it I was in the subbasement with piles of dirty laundry, clanging pipes, and rows of stretchers to keep me company. I went down countless corridors, up and down stair wells, and in and out of a hundred doors with huge warnings overhead to "Keep Out" before finally ending up across the street in Sloan-Kettering. I explained my problem to the guard on duty and he told

4

me that under the circumstances it would be easiest for me to take the outside route. He pointed to a large building on the corner of Sixty-seventh Street and First Avenue and told me that that was where I wanted to go. I had to admit that it took a certain amount of talent to miss an enire building, but then I'm not really famous for my fine sense of direction. Anyway, that did seem like the best plan, but it was seventeen degrees out there and our uniforms were hardly adequate in that kind of weather. So I asked him if that was the best idea he could come up with.

"No," he said, "if you go back to Memorial there's this yellow line. . . ." I wanted so badly to tell him what he could do with that routine, but, considering his size, I decided to brave the freezing temperatures instead.

Now the long trek between the two hospitals had become second nature to me, I thought as the elevator stopped on the mezzanine level. I walked down two more corridors and at last came to the final set of elevators that would take me up to Ewing 5.

I shifted my load and pushed the button. My arms were beginning to hurt and I was getting a permanent cleft in my chin from the Monopoly game, which had assumed a most unfortunate position some miles back. I couldn't help but think that the kids in Pediatrics knew what they were talking about when they referred to us as the "U-Haul-It" department. The green arrow lit up and the doors opened. Ozzie, the elevator operator, helped me on. "They've got you kids going early." He laughed. "Five, right?"

I nodded. "Where else?" I got out and deposited my load on the nearest available table. The scene was familiar enough: the pay phone with the usual long line formed in front of it; the T.V. blaring in the waiting area with no one watching it; and, as on every other Monday morning, the men eager to know if this week's movie was X-rated or not. I was always tempted to tell them that it was a really hot film for mature audiences only, but refrained from doing so for fear of causing a stampede. It's not that they were dirty old men exactly—they were just BORED! In the midst of this scene I felt a firm tap on my shoulder and, looking up, saw Mr. Mahoney, one of our livelier patients, giving me the high sign. I grabbed the *Playboy* magazine and raced after him. He was easily seventy years old, balding, with bright blue eyes, and his favorite pastime was trying to figure out if the femme fatale in the centerfold was "for real" or not. Mr. Mahoney was definitely not one of those who suffered from boredom.

"I see I'm in luck," he said, taking the magazine from me. "Did you check for the red marks like I taught you?" He laughed.

I wasn't what you'd call an authority on silicone shots and the telltale red marks that they

6

left. Needless to say, the nuns at Sacred Heart didn't teach us about such things. But to the best of my knowledge the young lady in question had left well enough alone. Mr. Mahoney was pleased about that and started walking toward the window at the end of the hall, explaining that "the light was better down there." He was joined by five or six of his friends, and I knew that at least for the next hour or so they'd be a very happy and thoroughly engrossed group of men. I glanced around and, seeing that most everybody was occupied in their various projects, decided that this would be as good a time as any to sneak over to the scale hidden behind the wall and check out my weight in privacy. Only five more pounds to go and then it was back to my napoleons and chocolate eclairs, which had been reluctantly forgone for the past month. Hospital scales have always been a real problem for me, but now they had become downright impossible. According to this I weighed 42. I mean it balanced, but it would take a mathematical genius to figure out what the 42 stood for. I didn't realize that I had been conducting an animated one-way conversation with myself until a voice from behind me said in a somewhat amused tone, "The weight is measured in kilos now instead of pounds. There's a chart beside you that should provide the answers." Of course, he was right and, feeling just a little embarrassed over my stupidity, I turned to thank him. He was tall, maybe six foot two, blond, with an athletic build, and was an incredibly good-looking boy. I guessed his age to be somewhere between eighteen and twenty-one. He came over and leaned on the scale.

"My name's Graham Banks," he said. "I was admitted yesterday."

I introduced myself and told him that I worked in the Recreation Department. He was full of questions, so having a conversation with him wasn't difficult. In fact, he was one of the friendliest people I'd ever met. He told me that he'd been headed for football camp only a few days before, but had ended up here instead.

"That's a bummer, isn't it?" The question seemed rhetorical, so I just nodded. We walked up and down the hall while he told me about school, his family, his friends, and I listened as he talked avidly of sports, which seemed to be his first love. Not a word was mentioned about what had brought him into the hospital in the first place, so I didn't ask. He asked me about my own family and my job, but his attention was constantly being diverted by the pretty nurses and one especially sexy social worker whose skirt was somewhere up in the region of no man's land. Granted, my life story was no thriller, but I thought he could've shown a little more interest just for the sake of being polite. I have to admit that my pride was beginning to suffer, and when our conversation finally resumed, what was left of it went right down the tubes.

"How old are you, anyway?" he asked.

Aha, I thought, the inevitable question has come. Usually it took a day or two before they asked. He was a mover all right.

"I'm twenty-two."

"Twenty-two! My God, I thought you were younger than that!"

Well, so much for the ego. His shock was so total that it was funny, but in that one reaction he made me feel as if I were not only over the hill but ready for retirement.

"Twenty-two," I assured him, "doesn't make me a candidate for the old folks' home. In fact, some people would consider it to be quite young."

But this didn't seem to make him feel any better. He just kept muttering, "Yeah, but twenty-two!"

This conversation was going nowhere, so I changed the subject back to him, and when I asked if he was in college yet, he said that he was.

"What year?"

He straightened, and then grinned. "Sophomore," he said.

The P.A. system was blaring my name throughout the hospital now, reminding me that as usual I was in the wrong place at the wrong time.

"Look, I've got to go," I told him, "but we'll be back to check on you, okay?"

"We?"

Brother, this one didn't miss a trick. "Barbara and Phyllis, my co-workers." I smiled. "Tall, blond . . . you'll like them."

We started walking toward the elevator.

"If it's okay, I'd like to come down to your department soon. They want me around here today, but maybe tomorrow."

"Any time," I said. "We're on the second floor of Memorial."

He left then and joined Mr. Mahoney and the others at the window.

I started back to the office knowing full well that I was going to catch it for being gone so long. Monday mornings were the most hectic of the week and our time was limited. There was the distribution of the activities schedule for all 550 patients, and sewing to be given out in both hospitals, as well as inviting people to the music recital in the afternoon. This last job was the most important, as our pianist was a temperamental soul who made it clear that he liked an audience of more than one.

On my way back I made a mental note to tell Phyllis and Barbara about Graham. If he was to be with us for long, which I doubted, it was important that he meet the younger kids. We kept a specially close eye on the teen-agers and people in their early twenties, maybe because they were so near our own age, or maybe because they made more of an effort to participate in our activities. I can't say for sure; probably a combination of both. We established a deep rapport with many of them because their stays at the hospital were usually long and readmissions for some were almost a certainty. They spent a lot of time in our office playing the guitar, singing, talking, and helping us with our work. For them it was a place to go and do what they pleased without being hassled. Once they became acclimated to the hospital and its routine they were pretty much free agents, roaming around in their jeans, not allowing themselves to be intimidated by where they were or why. They had a sense of belonging not only to us but especially to each other. It was a healthy atmosphere, one of give and take, and despite our various gripes the job was truly rewarding.

As I stood at the sink later that afternoon washing out the small vases for the night's flower distribution, a job we all detested, Barbara came to the door.

"Having fun?"

She could afford to make jokes, I thought. Her hands haven't been soaking in this foul Alcanox detergent for the past forty-five minutes. We had long ago decided to share the pit chores and this week it was my turn. She had also devised a plan of cutting cards to see who was going to do what and when—so far the only one benefiting from this little scheme was herself. Phyllis and I were convinced she had missed her calling: she would have been a wiz out in Las Vegas. We had decided, too, that her card-cutting and coin-flipping days were rapidly drawing to a close.

"How many admits do we have?" I asked, hoping that I had washed enough bottles.

"Oh, around 102."

"That's really not cute, Barb. Now, how many?"

Phyllis came to the door, laughing. "When are you going to stop believing everything she tells you?" She paused. "There are 106."

They beat a hasty retreat for obvious reasons and left me with umpteen bottles still to be done.

A few minutes later Phyllis returned, which was gutsy of her, I thought, and asked, "This twenty-year-old that you told us about, his name's Graham Banks?"

"Yeah, why?"

"That's funny. His admit slip says he's fifteen."

I dried my hands and took the slip from her. Sure enough, fifteen years old.

"Well, I'll be damned," I said. "I've been conned."

Graham was in for only five days, and not once did he mention what was wrong with him. He was such a live wire that we just naturally assumed he wasn't one of our sicker kids and let it go at that. Considering our experience with teen-agers we should've known better, but I suspect it was more wishful thinking on our part than anything else. He had by this time been adopted into the department and his energy, which was limitless, was put to good use by us. He was willing and even anxious to help out with some of the more menial tasks and this, of course, made him one of our favorites. Seeing him with the other patients, old and young alike, was incredible. He was a natural with people and could get them to do things when all other means of persuasion had failed. We never questioned his methods but he seemed to be particularly effective with the females. Keeping this in mind, I asked him one day as a favor to visit the sister of my dad's secretary, a Mrs. Bettie Egeler, who had just undergone radical head and neck surgery for cancer. She was a very special woman, and I had grown fond of her. I warned him that this type of surgery was disfiguring, and if he thought it would bother him, not to go, I'd understand. He said it made no difference to him and asked for her room number. They spent most of the day together, and when he returned later that afternoon he said, "That's one beautiful lady." He made a point of seeing her every day and I guess that's when I began to appreciate the type of boy he was.

During that week Graham became very close to us and it was with mixed emotions that we said good-by—glad that he was going home but knowing that life around the hospital was going to be duller without him. The possibility of his returning hadn't occurred to any of us.

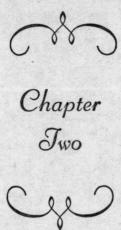

*Chapter
Two*

There were six of us who made up the staff of the Recreation Department: Michele, our supervisor; Kit, our assistant director and pediatric worker; Yolanda, our secretary; and Phyllis, Barbara, and myself. It was our function to reach the patients with our activities and to provide as normal and as pleasant an atmosphere as possible. Our philosophy about them was simple —as long as they're creating they are living, and as long as they're dealing with the positive they are focusing on life itself. Because they saw so much of us and knew that our time was theirs, they felt comfortable in asking us to do occasional favors for them and their families: anything from buying a birthday present to picking up a special lobster dinner at Oscar's. But once in a while these favors weren't all that routine, and, if this was the case, more often than not all hell would break loose.

On a fairly quiet Friday afternoon the three of us were in the office staining wood for the decoupage class the following day when a woman walked in with a child in her arms. She explained in halting English that her husband had just returned from surgery and that she was anxious to see him but had no one to leave the baby with. She said he'd spoken frequently about the department and had told her often how very fond he was of us. Well, naturally, with flattery like that, we offered to take the kid. *That* was our first mistake. Our second came a few minutes later when Albert, a young boy whose father was being discharged that evening and taken back to Iran, appeared. He had a squirming bundle of black and brown fur in his arms and asked if we'd mind watching it for a little while. Like idiots we agreed, and now here we were with a two-year-old kid named Montague and a six-week-old puppy named Horatio. It's hard to say just how long it took before our office hit the skids, but it happened with remarkable speed and destruction was total. God knows, we did everything in our power to keep Montague happy but he was far too energetic for us. He finger-painted the walls, broke the crayons, stuck pieces of puzzles up his nose, and, when he became bored, ran up and down the second-floor corridor yelling, "Catch me—ha-ha—catch me!"

"Cute kid," Barbara said, reaching for the cards. She was showing her usual calm brilliance in the face of disaster, I thought. We cut, and naturally Barb came up with an ace, while mine was a five and Phyllis, bless her heart, produced a two. She took off muttering a few mild obscenities and, after her third near-miss, stuck her head in the door swearing, "I'll catch him all right and when I do I'm going to nail his suspenders to the wall."

"You'll make a wonderful mother someday," Barb said, "so warm, patient, understanding. . . ."

For all the kidding we were giving Phyllis about her problem, Horatio was more than making it up to us by going "dumpy by" (Montague's description, not ours) at an alarming rate on our floor, and as fast as we'd clean it up he'd deposit another load somewhere else. It just seemed simpler in the long run to leave it and clean it up when we were sure he was through. So far our calculations had been 100 per cent wrong. Needless to say, neither of them was making great strides in gaining our love and affection, so we settled back figuring that sooner or later they were bound to poop out.

When Graham arrived at the door we were beyond registering surprise. As a matter of fact, we were beyond registering anything at all. He looked unbelievingly around the room and chuckled. "Redecorating the office? It's got kind of a nice touch, sort of early American dog. . . ."

"Don't say it—and watch where you step," Barbara warned as he came in.

"What happened?" he asked. We laughed and pointed over to Horatio, who was huddled over in the corner with Montague, sound asleep. Looking at them, one would never suspect that they were the culprits.

"Well, there's always disaster relief," Graham commented, putting his feet up on the table.

"And you're it," I said, pressing a paper towel into his hands.

He made a classic remark about not having come by to see us for this purpose, and I made the bad mistake then of telling him that the way he dished it out he should feel right at home cleaning it up. He smiled, and looked at me. His eyes had a nasty glint in them, and, leaning over, he scooped up some "dumpy by," holding it dangerously close to my face. Having been brought up with three brothers, I recognized the look and, not waiting to see if the implied threat would indeed become a reality, took off down the hall. I ducked behind a door that led down to the lobby and waited . . . and waited . . . and waited. My heart was pounding, my jaws were clenched, and my palms were beginning to sweat. Classic symptoms of nerves, I thought. I checked the stair well—nothing. I listened for voices—nothing. Maybe I'd misread the look. No, I had seen it too many times. Voices . . . footsteps, getting closer. My hand was now a fist. The door opened and I jumped out.

"Aha! Gotcha!"

"No doubt about it!"

The voice came from a doubled-over figure in

white accompanied by two of his colleagues, and behind them, leaning against the wall in hysterics, were Barbara and Graham. "Dear God!" I blurted out as the doctor straightened carefully, holding his hand over his stomach.

"Now I know why your friends let us go first," he said. "We thought they were just being polite."

"Uh, no," I mumbled, "just smart. I hope I didn't hurt you."

He assured me that he was all right. "Stunned," he said, "would sum it up better."

He didn't look familiar and, trying to be pleasant, not to mention salvaging my job, I asked him if he was new on staff. "Today, as a matter of fact," he said, dodging and weaving past me. "I'm on the Gynecology service."

Why, I asked myself, did you have to belt one of them? If there was one group of doctors I didn't want to be on the wrong end of, that was certainly it.

He glanced at his cohorts and then back at me. "I'll be seeing you again, Mari Brady."

I took my name tag off and put it in my pocket. "Don't count on it," I muttered.

Barbara and Graham were waiting back in the office, obviously still enjoying the comedy of errors that had just taken place.

"Nice going, Ace." Graham grinned. "You should've seen the look on your face."

I laughed. "You should've seen the look on his!"

It was close to five when the dynamic duo were picked up by their respective owners with apologies for having left them so long. Now that things had settled down we turned our attention to Graham, who as yet hadn't explained what he was even doing back at the hospital.

"I'm scheduled for surgery on Monday—a lymph node operation," he said.

Barbara, Phyllis, and I looked at each other and stiffened. We knew that this was a major procedure performed to stop the spread of cancer. It was the first indication we had that there was something seriously wrong with him. We were careful not to say anything until we knew how he felt. So far, he hadn't said a word—his feelings were his own and we had to respect that. It would have been unfair for us to overreact. As I watched him walk calmly around the room, picking things up and placing them gently back on the table, I couldn't help thinking that he must have known.

Graham turned around to face us. "It's crummy, huh?"

"Yeah, crummy," Barbara said, her voice edged with anger.

The phone rang and I answered it. It was Linda, a nurse from Memorial 8, looking for Graham. I got my coat, since it was quitting time for me anyway, and went upstairs with him. His mother was waiting outside in the hall, looking slightly miffed, but he took no notice as he went past her into the room. It was a single, and he wasn't too thrilled about that. He much preferred to be with people. Throwing his coat on the chair, he stretched out on the bed.

"Any kids on this floor?" he asked.

"Pete Davidson in 840. He's twenty-three and doesn't have any visitors."

Graham sat up. "Why not?"

"He lives in Florida and there are some family problems."

"That's rough," he said. "I'd like to meet him now if it's okay with you."

Fortunately I didn't have any objections because before I had a chance to answer he jumped up and took off toward Pete's room. I introduced the boys and, seeing that they hit it off immediately, I left, with a promise to come and see Graham first thing on Monday morning before surgery.

When I arrived Monday he was asleep on the stretcher and the orderly was preparing to take him up to the O.R. I rode with him as far as the twelfth floor, and just as the elevator doors opened Graham woke up. "You made it," he said, smiling.

"I said I would."

He nodded and fell back to sleep.

The operation lasted all morning and he remained in Recovery until late that night. I didn't see him until the following afternoon. His mother, who was sitting beside his bed, went out to have

23

a cigarette in the waiting room, leaving us alone to talk. He seemed to need that and really opened up. In fact, during the course of the next few days our conversations covered nearly every subject from school to Africa. He expressed concern that he was missing so much work and was convinced that he was going to be the oldest living sophomore in history.

"Of course," he admitted, "it would probably help if my friends and I quit cutting classes to go up to the mountains."

"Perish the thought. That's probably doing wonders for your grades."

"*Very* funny."

Then, quite suddenly, he became serious. "I have a dream," he said; "more than anything else in the world I want to spend a summer in Africa —to see the land, the people and how they live, but the animals"—he smiled—"they're what I want to see most."

I had been to the Congo a few years before as a member of an international youth group called "Up With People." We traveled throughout the world trying to create a bond of understanding among the young people of different nations. It was very idealistic on our part, but in this day and age of cynicism there was nothing wrong with that. We got our ideas across in a two-hour musical show, sung mostly in the native language. When I told him this, though, I'm not sure that he believed me. He kept saying, "You're joking, aren't you?"

I assured him that I was on the level and, just to prove it, the next afternoon I brought him in my drum that a native had made and a beautifully illustrated book on Africa. We spent hours going through the book and I watched as he read and devoured all the information that he could. He asked me to tell him everything about my trip. Africa is a difficult place to describe only because when you're there you feel and absorb so much that it is impossible to put it all into words. But since it was so important to him, I gave as vivid a picture as possible, starting with a sunrise over the Sahara Desert—the brilliant pink, orange, and yellow sky interspersed with small white clouds, the sand below shifting quickly, giving the impression that we were watching a large body of water. I told him of the lush forests; the huts lining the streets into the main city with the near-naked children playing outside; our trip down the Congo River and the incredible sunset that cast a mystic, almost eerie glow over the hills and villages bordering it. These same waters, I continued, were where the natives fished—

"With their bare hands?" Graham interrupted.

"No," I said, and explained how they drove huge poles between the rocks and built a scaffold-like structure where large hand-woven conical traps were lowered into the rapids. It was a daring procedure, but apparently a necessary one.

He gave a low whistle. "Hasn't anybody ever told them about a rod and reel?" he asked.

"Why don't you write them a letter?"

"Okay, okay." He laughed. "It just seems a little complicated, that's all. So go on."

I described the Grand Marché where you could barter for ivory, copper, paintings, and wood carvings—and finally the Africans themselves: their dress, their traditions, and the way they lived; a friendly determined people who possessed a fierce pride.

He hung on every word. He just couldn't get enough. As the day wore on, though, I began to notice a funny expression on his face and a yearning developed in his voice, as though, if given half a chance, he'd bolt right out of bed, purchase a ticket, and take off for the wilds of Africa. As far as I was concerned, nothing was beyond the realm of possibility with this kid, so I thought it wise to warn him of the country's pitfalls— and believe me, there were plenty.

When we first arrived there after a long and tiring flight there were two things uppermost in our minds—food and sleep. We were met and taken to a large hall where we were seated at long wooden tables with benches. In front of us were plates filled with a reddish brown meat and white balls floating in a thick creamy sauce. I caught one of the natives by the sleeve. "Qu'est-ce que c'est?" I asked, pointing to the meat.

"La viande de singe." He waited while I quickly translated. "The meat of monkey—oh my!"

"Et ça?" I asked again, pointing to the balls in the sauce. His grin widened and the words this time were unfamiliar, which made me a little nervous. I climbed over the bench and walked the mile back along a dirt road to a little store we had passed on our way in from town. No way, I thought, am I eating anything that had been swinging from a tree, and as for the other stuff, if I couldn't translate it, you could bet your life I wasn't going to eat it. I bought enough Hershey bars and Coke to last through the night, figuring that breakfast had to be an improvement over dinner. Unfortunately my optimism was short-lived when the next morning we found lying on a dish the biggest mother sardines you ever saw staring up at us with their beady little eyes. For a meat-and-potatoes girl this was more than I could take, so I dug a hole in the ground with my foot, picked my little friends up by the tail, and gave them a quick and proper burial. This time when I went back to the store I stocked up on enough Hersheys and Coke to last me a month.

Graham was laughing now. "Sounds like the garbage you get here," he said. "So go on."

I couldn't believe he wanted to hear more. Monkey meat and sardines would've been more

27

than enough to kill my interest. So I told him about the lizards that crept through the holes in the wall, the scorpions that made it necessary to put your cot in the middle of the room, and the community bathroom that was without a doubt the biggest and most embarrassing inconvenience of all. It was probably the only one of its kind on the entire continent, but leave it to us to find it. I mean to say, everyone shared it—men, women, you name it and they used it. The Africans didn't think twice about it but we did. Somehow doing your thing with the threat of a man walking in on you wasn't terribly appealing. We thought we were being so smart by posting guards outside until we realized that the only word we knew in Lingala, *mbote,* meant "hello." Of course, they thought we were the friendliest tourists going and continued to pop in on us at the damndest times.

"Believe me," I said, "it didn't pay to lose your sense of humor."

Graham picked up the drum, tracing the outline of it with his finger, and, still laughing, said, "This thing's almost as big as you are. Were you able to bring back anything else?"

"Yeah," I said, "thirty-two cavities."

Of course, he thought this was terrific, but then only Graham would. Recounting some of these episodes, though, seemed to do the trick and Cape Cod, which he loved, was beginning to look better and better. If I had to pick a time when we started becoming so close, this would be it. I suspect the fact that he was confined to bed and couldn't run all over God's green earth had something to do with that, but I was glad that we had this time to really get to know each other.

A few days later the doctors gave him permission to get up and move around. "Mild exercise" is the way they explained it to him. But he was impatient and decided that walking up and down the hall wasn't enough. He began doing push-ups "to get in shape." His mother and doctor didn't see it that way and he got a severe reprimand from them both, which upset him. Later that day we got a message that he wanted to see us.

"I want to go over and visit my friends and the nurses on Ewing 5, but I doubt they'll let me go by myself," he said. "I really caught it from my doctor and my mom today for overdoing it, but if I'm with you they'll probably let me go." He paused. "I just want out of this room!"

It was unbelievable that he felt this well, but he assured us that he was fine, so we checked with the nurses and they said okay. When we asked him if he needed a wheel chair his answer was a firm and emphatic "NO!" He was adamant about not having any help, so we just let it drop. Except that he held his side when he walked you wouldn't have suspected that he had just undergone major surgery. We had to admit that he was in remarkable condition. We stayed over there until nearly dinnertime and Graham really enjoyed the visit. He perked up considerably and seemed to have forgotten all about the bawling out he had received earlier. On our way back he was unusually quiet and, noticing this, I turned to ask him if he was all right. He wasn't there. Barb and I retraced our steps to where we had last seen him, but we couldn't find him anywhere. I had visions of him lying somewhere with broken stitches or some such thing and I was really frightened. We went back to the X-ray Department, midway between Memorial and Ewing, chose two chairs that were strategically perfect, and waited for him. I couldn't help cursing to myself that if he was pulling a disappearing act I'd murder him. We settled back and started talking to those around us, passing the time until he showed. We were there for only about two minutes when we saw him emerge from the elevator. He really did look funny with his open bathrobe, T shirt, and cut-off pajama bottoms, peeping around corners, looking from left to right, making sure that the coast was clear, and slinking along the wall to avoid detection. Of course, these very maneuvers attracted the stares of inquisitive onlookers in the first place and prompted Mrs. Shapiro, a visitor, to comment on what nice legs he had. At the rate he was going it would take him about ten seconds before he crossed our path and we could nab him.

"Going somewhere?" we asked as we each grabbed an arm. He could tell we weren't altogether pleased about this latest prank.

"Sorry, you guys," he said. But his apology wasn't terribly convincing.

"In a pig's eye you are!" I shot back.

When we arrived on eight it was just in time to see his belongings being moved down the hall to a semiprivate room. He was happy about this, as he truly hated being alone. He was glad to see that "Ole Jack" and he were roommates again, along with Pete, who had been moved the day before. Jack was an older man, maybe sixty or so, who had shared a room with Graham on Ewing 5, and had confided to me then that "he's a good kid, a great kid in fact, he's just got too damn many friends." Jack was referring to the times when a group of them would hitch a ride from northern New Jersey into the city with Mrs. Banks to visit Graham. So far, during this admission he hadn't felt up to that many visitors and our department had been spared, but we all knew that their coming was inevitable and braced ourselves for the onslaught ahead. It came sooner than we expected. There must have been at least fifteen of them, and it was par for the course to see six or seven of the boys popping their heads in and out of the patents' rooms taking orders for pizza, hot dogs, and beer, collecting the money upon delivery. The radiators were turned into makeshift ovens to keep the food warm and that floor quickly gained the reputation of the place to go for good food, good drink, and good times. Even Jack got into the swing of things and started thinking of the kids as "not so bad after all."

But the eighth floor returned to normal when Graham, whose recovery had been quick, was discharged the following week.

Chapter
Three

For Graham, surgery wasn't enough. It was imperative that he come to clinic once a week for chemotherapy, another way of arresting the disease with powerful drugs. Because of the severe side effects, it was the part of his treatment he hated most. He suffered terrible nausea, ulcerated sores in his mouth, and—the final blow—the loss of his hair.

Up until now he had found it difficult to open up and discuss his illness, and no one pushed him. Some people were able to talk about it freely right from the beginning, while others took longer to accept the reality. Graham had had nearly two months now to get his head together, and he wanted to know why it was still necessary to continue the chemotherapy. He made it plain to his doctor that he wanted to be told straight. So his doctor explained to him that it was crucial in order to check the growth of tumors that were forming in his lungs.

When he came down to see us after the appointment he said how grateful he was for his doctor's honesty, and how relieved that at least he now knew where he stood. He told us about the talk and said, "It's not so much that you're afraid of dying, as knowing the crap you have to go through in order to live."

We sat and listened while he said, "It's a gamble, I suppose, and you do what you have to in order to lick it. There's just no choice, no choice at all." He stayed with us for quite a while, not saying a word, and when he finally got up to leave he looked at us and said, "The thing about being in this place is knowing that you're not alone. People care—that helps, you know? It helps a lot."

These were the times when our job wasn't all fun and games and we found it necessary to get out and walk for a while, just to think. It was nearly dinnertime, and Barbara was on a diet, so she stayed in the office with her yogurt while Phyllis and I went down to the river. As we walked, I thought about when I first applied for the job at Memorial. My reasons were simple enough: I hated secretarial school, and I needed the money. After a year of typing and shorthand it was becoming painfully evident to everyone that my talents did not lie in this area. But now I had to admit that maybe my reasons weren't as simple as all that. Our family had known the pain of losing someone to cancer, and buried deep inside of me was a hatred for this disease that went beyond words. At Memorial there was a bond between the staff and the patients, a feeling of hope that one day cancer would be cured.

I leaned against the railing and looked out over the water. Phyllis turned and faced me.

"Are you thinking about what Graham said?"

"I guess, among other things."

"He got to you, didn't he?" she asked.

Phyllis was right, he had gotten to me, but all the kids did in one way or another. Graham, though, was someone who had become very special to me and what he had said that afternoon made me realize just how sick he was. This hurt—but we had to try and find acceptance and faith just as the kids did, and to learn to share ourselves openly and honestly with them.

"Sometimes," I said, "you feel so damn helpless ; that's the part I can't stand."

Phyllis looked out toward the city. "I guess we all have to fight it in our own way," she said softly. "The doctors and nurses give what they've got up here"—she pointed to her head—"and the rest of us can only give our love—that's all we have."

It was true. We saw the doctors there from the crack of dawn to sometimes really late at night, and it wasn't unusual to see a nurse run into the hospital on her day off just to check on a patient. People became involved. Not everyone, of course, because in any large institution you're going to find a few bimbos, but thank God, they were scarce.

Phyllis started to laugh, and I looked at her as if she had rocks in her head. Up to this point I hadn't seen the humor in the conversation.

"What's so funny?" I asked.

"I was just remembering the night we saw that doctor in a tuxedo wheeling his patient down the hall and how he drove that thing like a bat out of hell. Remember the look on Mrs. Prescott's face? She was loving every minute of it. For once she was giving the orders and he was following them. A nice change of pace for a patient, I'd say."

She paused and looked at me. "If you were a patient here, would you be able to take it? Would you have that kind of will to live?"

I'd thought about that question often and now it was my turn to laugh. "Let's put it this way. Last year I went to a doctor for a sore throat, and when he strongly recommended a tonsillectomy, I was on the first plane down to Florida."

"That's really pathetic!"

"I know."

As we stood there I thought back to Graham's words. *Care*—"People care," he had said, and he was right.

We saw the best of it and the worst of it. If they lived we were a part of their victory, and if they died we had to learn to deal with it—to pick up from where they left off and, no matter how hard it was for us, go on. You see, we were working with kids who lived life more fully and with more courage than anybody we'd ever met, and we felt as if we owed them the best that we had to give.

We watched the water in silence. Then Phyllis moved, snapping me out of my own private thoughts.

"Have you ever tried explaining to friends why our job means so much to us?" she asked. "I mean so that they *really* understand?"

"Sure I've tried, but most of my friends thought I was becoming too involved and shutting myself off from them. How can you expect them to know what we're doing here, or how much people like Graham mean to us, when they haven't worked with these kids? We're dealing with feelings, Phyll, and sometimes you can't explain them. Let's face it, cancer isn't exactly a pleasant topic of conversation at a dinner party and most people are uncomfortable talking about it. Besides, I've found that it's easier to keep my mouth shut and just try to live what I've learned. Do you see what I'm getting at?"

"Yes, I know," she said, "but I still wish that there was a way we could make them understand."

As we walked back to the hospital I thought, yes, we get depressed. We cried because sometimes we really ached inside. But we had each other, Phyllis, Barbara, and I. We had other staff members who were good friends; and we had our families, who would listen when things got to be too much. And when we went away, it was always out of the city where we could try to forget and live our own lives. In a way we were living in two different worlds: separate, and yet one always giving to the other. We couldn't ask for much more.

Christmas was only two weeks away and the days had a way of running into one another with little consideration for those of us trying to get the hospital decorated, the windows painted, the packages wrapped, and the daily activities organized with some semblance of sanity. It was perfectly normal to see us running through the halls carrying ladders, waving paintbrushes, and stuffing our faces with the chocolate candy that had been given to us as presents from the patients. You've heard of the old saying "He who eats it today wears it tomorrow." Well, for us truer words were never spoken. Inside of a week we all had the worst cases of adolescent acne imaginable. Phyllis came in one morning in an absolute stupor.

"Look at this," she said in disgust, staring at her reflection in the mirror. "They just popped up overnight, and I've forgotten how to get rid of the little devils."

We survived the acne, got everything finished

on time, and with great relief were ready for the distribution of gifts to the patients who had to remain in the hospital. Most were allowed to go home on pass for the holidays, but for those who couldn't we had two Santa Clauses, ten elves, eight carolers, and two carts piled high with brightly wrapped gifts to help make their day a little happier. We split up into two teams, one to go to Memorial and the other to Ewing. Phyllis and I were put in charge of the latter, and it was during Michele's last-minute instructions that we snuck over to clinic to see Graham and the other kids, sure that whatever she had to say we'd heard it all before.

We got back to the office just as Michele was wrapping up her little talk, and when she asked if there were any questions we assured her that we had everything under control. Now, whenever Phyllis and I did anything, no matter how simple it was, you could bet on something getting screwed up. Rarely did we have any situation "under control," and that's why, after we finished over in Ewing, I had this nagging feeling that things had gone entirely too smoothly. On our way back I happened to mention casually that I was sure somewhere along the line we'd made a colossal mistake.

"Don't say that!" Phyllis said. "This is the first time that everything went off without a hitch—so stop worrying, will you?"

"Doesn't that make you nervous?" I asked.

"Yeah, a little. That's why I don't want to think about it." She laughed.

I shut up then. No sense in getting worked up over some dumb feeling that I had, right? When we got back to the office we discovered that the others who were doing the distribution in Memorial were still up on the floors. Phyllis suggested that I go up and tell them that we were through and would like to go home, while she cleaned up and put away the remaining gifts.

I met them on the sixth floor and stopped dead in my tracks when I saw Santa giving to a woman a package identical to the ones that we had given to thirty men over in Ewing not more than twenty minutes ago. Somebody had goofed and I was betting on Phyllis and me. I walked up and stood beside the lady's bed and waited while she ripped away the paper.

Please let it be after-shave lotion, I prayed.

"Perfume," she exclaimed excitedly. "How lovely!"

I made it down to the second floor in record time and stood at the door to our office trying to catch my breath. Phyllis took one look at me and knew immediately that we were in trouble. I told her about the mix-up and, showing great intelligence, we decided that something had to be done before Michele found out.

Phyllis started to pace. "The most important thing is not to panic," she said.

"Right," I agreed. "Panicking is out." How I wished Barbara were here with us now, but she had been smart and left the day before for Pennsylvania. She was by far the most unflappable of the three of us, and without her we promptly fell into such a state that we didn't even notice Graham and Pete standing out in the hall.

"What's with you two?" Graham asked.

We explained what had happened. We had to stall Michele because we were afraid if she found out that we had given thirty bottles of perfume to men she'd kill us. Pete came up with what seemed like a fairly simple solution.

"Mar, you and Graham go back upstairs and stall Michele while Phyll and I go and exchange the gifts."

I asked him if he had any brilliant ideas on how we were to do this, figuring anything short of breaking Santa's leg wouldn't be drastic enough to get us out of this one.

"I don't know, fake a stroke or something." He chuckled. "You look like you're only minutes away from one, anyway."

So, while Phyllis and Pete returned to Ewing with some after-shave lotion, Graham and I went back up to the sixth floor. When we got there we heard exclamations of disgust and pure frustration down the hall. Looking over, we saw much to our delight that the wheels of the cart

43

were stuck quite firmly in the grooves of the elevator. I felt as if we had just been given a reprieve and we watched as one mishap after another occurred. Graham loved every minute of it.

"What a shame," he whispered. "Think we ought to help?"

"Move, and I'll break your arm."

We were able to buy the forty-five minutes that we so desperately needed and we arrived back at the office slightly ahead of the others. Pete and Phyllis were sitting there waiting for us, looking a little peaked but on the whole okay.

"Nice work," Phyll said, "but what took you so long?"

"The cart kept getting stuck," Graham said, smiling. "They were getting kind of hostile up there."

"By the way," I asked, "what did you do with the perfume?"

"Are you kidding, I let them keep it," Phyllis said. "Besides, they were really impressed that we remembered their wives at Christmas."

"Aren't you two the lucky ones." Pete grinned. "What would you do without us?"

Under normal circumstances that would've been a loaded question, but today I had to admit that we would have been lost without them.

Michele came over then and thanked us for doing such a "magnificent" job, giving each of us a hug as Pete and Graham watched. Rolling their eyes and laughing, they made for the door.

"Merry Christmas, you guys, and keep the faith!"

Chapter
Four

Barbara, Phyllis, and I tried to get over to clinic as often as possible because there we saw the patients who were either in remission or cured and had come back for routine checkups and treatment. Since we worked in the hospital, it was hard for us to remember sometimes how well many people were doing because the kids that we really grew to know and love were the ones who came back for repeat admissions. This tended to give us an unrealistic and somewhat pessimistic view of the disease. In clinic, though, we could see for ourselves the numerous successes, the living testimony of what Memorial stood for, and it helped reaffirm our own faith in the work being done there. We saw Graham each week and he seemed to be doing well, but then in early February it was decided that another operation was necessary. He was scheduled to be readmitted on the seventh, but at the last minute the admitting office called his home to say that there were no available beds on his doctor's service, and that his surgery would have to be postponed for a week. He had been emotionally prepared to come back in. He told me once that the worst part of going to the hospital were the days before when you did nothing but wait and worry—"scared to death of what they might find."

"It's the getting there that's the trick," he said. "Once you're in, it's okay." His mother said that he flipped out when he heard of the delay. Now he would have more time to think about his surgery, and the torment was more than he could stand. When the message came he stood yelling at those around him and finally, in pure frustration, gave the living room couch one good swift kick. With his family and friends he watched in amazement as it collapsed. Whirling around in anger, he ran from the back of the house toward the glen. One of his friends, Jason, went after him.

"God, no!" he heard Graham scream. "Why?"

Jason caught up with him. "Don't do this," he begged. "It's no good." Graham looked at him, threw his wig on the ground, and said, "Get the hell out of here, Jason, I'm warning you!"

"I won't, Graham!"

They fought, rolling down into the freezing water of the stream below. If nothing else, it calmed Graham down.

"Come on," Jason urged, "let's go before we freeze our butts off."

Graham picked up his wig, and the boys went back to the house. His mother was still standing by the couch when they returned and, seeing the incredulous look on her face, he managed a smile and said, "Sorry about that, Mom, but you said we needed a new one, anyway."

She looked at him and laughed. "That's very sporting of you!"

He shrugged. "I just hope the next one is sturdier than this," he said, nudging the couch with his foot. "I mean, one little kick and"—he snapped his fingers—"gone."

Phyllis and I had just finished putting the final touches to the decorations for the Valentine's party that night and were getting ready to go out for dinner when Michele announced that she wanted us back in the office in fifteen minutes. It seemed she was short of help and needed us to assist with the inviting. Now if we had been smart, or even thinking, for that matter, we would have forgone the pizza that had been uppermost in our minds all day and settled for "chicken quickie" in the cafeteria. But no, like fools we ran two blocks, inhaled four slices of pizza with extra cheese, drank two large cups of Pepsi, and made it back in the allotted fifteen minutes.

We took the piano down to the auditorium, assigned the volunteers their floors for inviting, checked the sound in the microphone, made sure there was enough room for the wheel chairs and stretchers, and then collapsed, exhausted, in the nearest available chairs. We saw Graham strolling through the lobby, and with him was Bobby Walters, a boy who had just been admitted a few days before. They pulled up two chairs and sat beside us.

"Another swinging party, eh?" Graham laughed. "I brought Bobby along—he's never been to one of these things."

"Lucky devil," Phyllis mumbled.

Kit, our assistant director, came over then and told us that three more floors in Memorial still had to be invited, and asked if we'd do it. She left before we had a chance to say no.

"Phyllis," I said, "I can't move," and looked over my shoulder to find her just staring at me.

"Well, let me tell you *I'm* not feeling too terrific myself."

The boys looked at us with genuine concern. "What's wrong with you two anyway? You look awful." I was reluctant to tell them what the problem was, knowing full well they'd never let us live it down, so I tried to put it as delicately as possible. "Touch of indigestion," I said, getting up, "and it would be wise of you to keep all smart remarks to yourself." Their reaction was as I suspected it would be, and I shot them a look that in polite language simply said, "Can it!" Phyllis informed them that if they weren't doing anything, which they weren't, they could

help with the inviting. So we took off—or maybe
I should say Graham and Bobby did. Phyll and
I just sort of slowly brought up the rear.

When the party was over, the boys took pity
on our condition, helped us clean up, and even
went so far as to bring the piano back to the
office for us.

While we were in the elevator on our way up
to the eighth floor, Bobby said, "Listen, I forgot
to tell you that Schultzy wants you to stop by
the room. He says he's got a surprise for you."

I laughed. "I just bet he has."

Mr. Schultz was a tiny seventy-eight-year-old
German with a longish crew cut that gave one
the impression that he had just backed into a
light socket. He was a strange old bird who
climbed into bed with women in the middle of
the night. (That in itself is quite normal, but
definitely frowned upon while in the hospital.)
He wrote letters on toilet paper, walked up and
down the halls incessantly to keep his bowels
moving, and, the night before, had insisted on
shining his shoes with the chocolate eclair that
we had given him. So when the elevator doors
opened and we saw Schultzy standing there with
a plastic bag over his head I can't really say that
it shocked us.

"The old boy's gone bananas," Phyllis whispered.

He slipped his arm around my waist, deftly
removed the platsic bag from his head, and said,

"I take shower. All clean. Now we make love, yah?" He smiled and pinched my cheek.

"Not now, Mr. Schultz."

"Try it, you might like it," Graham suggested as he moved away.

"Yah, we go now," Mr. Schultz agreed, his frog eyes growing larger.

"No, really, I'm just not in the mood."

I thought, God, that's not what I mean at all! I looked around for help, but found none. Even William, the elevator operator, was still standing there waiting to see how I'd get out of this one.

"Come, come," Schultzy coaxed, steering me down the hall.

I'm not ready for this, I thought, shooting a pleading look at Graham. He came over, put his arm around my shoulders, and pulled me away.

"She has a headache," he said.

I looked at him, not believing what I'd just heard.

"Now, that was original," I whispered.

He laughed. "I could've told him you had gas!"

"*Zut!*" Mr. Schultz swore, breaking into our conversation. "If you veren't feeling vell, you should have said so!" He walked away hitting himself on the head, muttering that he'd simply have to find someone else.

So far this had not been one of my better nights and I decided to get out of there before something else happened. Before I left I asked

Graham if he knew yet when his surgery was to be scheduled.

"Tomorrow," he said, taking his arm from my shoulders. "It's my lungs."

He was taken up to the O.R. early the next morning before we had a chance to see him and we found the waiting unbearable. We kept busy by doing the sewing distribution, giving decoupage lessons, and visiting, anything to help make the time pass more quickly. Around one o'clock Barbara and I went down to the lobby to check at the desk to see if he was in Recovery yet. Mrs. Banks, shaking and near tears, was sitting on one of the couches surrounded by Graham's friends. We went over and sat down beside her.

"The doctor was just here," she said. "They couldn't get it all." She paused. "The prognosis is very bad."

There was nothing to say, everything sounded so stupid and trite. Somehow the full impact of her words refused to sink in. She took my hand and we sat there in silence. I looked at Barb and then around at the boys. They hardly seemed like the same group. This was a lot for them to take at fifteen. Jason was pacing up and down in front of us.

"Where's the Recovery room?" he asked.

"Up on eleven," Barbara said, "but visitors aren't allowed up there."

He turned on her, his dark eyes flashing. "I

don't give a damn if it's allowed or not," he said, "because Graham's going to know that we're here with him!"

He left, and we didn't try to stop him. We were sure that if there was a way to get in he'd find it, and he did. He stayed with Graham until the nurses brought him down to his room later that night. I waited for everyone to leave before going up to see Graham. He was awake and very relaxed. When I asked how he felt he said, "Doing okay, Mar," and gave me the thumbs-up sign. I guess I felt relief at that point that he wasn't apprehensive or in great pain, and just seeing him in such good spirits made my own fears disappear. The doctor's prognosis began to fade from my memory. Whether Graham knew or not, I don't know—he never said a word.

Pete was readmitted a few days later for chemotherapy, and the boys spent a lot of time together catching up on all that had happened since they had last seen each other.

Graham remarked to me one day that he couldn't understand how Pete's parents could stay away. "Did you know," he said, "that Mr. Davidson had promised to come with him on this trip, but begged off at the last minute because of business?" He slammed his fist on the bed. "If they only had some idea of what it was like to be here. It's scary, Mar, and no one should be alone—no one!"

"There's not much of an explanation, Graham, not all parents are like yours. . . ." We turned around and saw Pete standing at the door. He came in and sat down on the bed. "Mom and Dad are divorced and married again with families of their own now, and I don't really belong to either of them any more." Staring out the window, he said, "It's funny. I really love my half sisters like they were a part of me. But my parents figure that since I'm sick, well, it's just better if I keep my distance."

I sat and listened. It wasn't our place to judge why this happened, but we saw it all too often and it tore us up inside. We had one nineteen-year-old boy who had been sick for three years and, abandoned by his family, he had said, "I'm a burden to everyone. It would be better if I just up and croaked." If it hadn't been for the care and concern of the other kids, he said, he would have stopped treatments and "quit trying." So I had to agree with Graham: it was impossible to understand. I got up and left the boys alone to talk.

While the second floor was under construction for our new hospital we made it a practice to stay out of the office as much as possible. It was really a matter of survival more than anything else. Every time we did go in, some damn pipe would come careening through the walls or a blowtorch would cut a hole dangerously close to where we were sitting, and the nonstop drilling was beginning to drive us crazy. But it wasn't until our secretary, Yolanda, was nearly wiped out twice "by mistake" that we decided it was definitely safer to stay away until after four, which left those of us on the late shift with a lot of extra work to do and threw our programs slightly out of whack. That night Barbara and I were preparing the following morning's activities when we heard the elevator stop on our floor and a multitude of voices heading for our office. There at the door, led by Pete, Graham, and Bobby, stood nearly twenty-five people.

"We're here for Bingo," Pete announced, moving aside to let the crowd pass into the room.

Barbara grabbed him by the arm and whispered, "You know that we had to cancel the program because the volunteer office was torn down this morning and that we're left without any help. Besides," she said through clenched teeth, "you hate Bingo!"

"I know," Pete said, giving her a little hug, "but we didn't want you to get lonely."

"How thoughtful."

In a matter of minutes we were running a combination Bingo game and short-order restaurant. ". . . Any coffee? . . . How about a Pepsi? . . . Where are the cookies?"

58

After the game had been going on for nearly an hour I went and stood against the counter, wondering how the peace and quiet of our office had turned into a zoo. I stared into the goldfish bowl. Right now they were the sanest things in the room. *Ugly*—but sane.

Graham came over to get something to drink. I glanced at him sideways. "I thought you were supposed to be taking it easy. Who'd you con this time?"

"One of the nurses." He laughed. "She's new, kind of cute, and uh, she doesn't know me that well yet."

"Obviously," I said, walking back to join the others.

"Bingo! Bingo! I've got Bingo!" yelled Mrs. Schmidt, the resident motor mouth, who had been grating on our nerves all night.

"Hot spit!" Graham muttered, just loud enough for all of us to hear him. His comment broke everyone up, but she ignored this as she came running up to me with her dyed red hair, pointed speckled eyeglasses, shocking-pink kimono, and, as a finishing touch, a pair of gold slippers that curled up at the ends.

"Listen, honey," she said, cracking her gum in my face, "I want that Chanel No. 5 hidden up there in that cabinet." She pointed with surprising accuracy to where we kept special gifts for birthdays and anniversaries.

"I'm sorry, but that's not a Bingo prize," I explained.

"Now, listen, I want that bottle of perfume! Are you going to give it to me or not?"

What I wanted to give her would have gotten me fired, and when I continued to protest she took my arm and guided me rather forcefully across the room.

"Listen, sweetie, that stuff turns my hubby on. Know what I mean?" She poked me in the ribs and winked at me as if I were some sort of dense nitwit.

"I know what you mean," I assured her with a sarcastic wink of my own.

I couldn't take any more of this, so I gave her the perfume, hoping that she'd grab it and take a powder, but she didn't. Instead, she went and sat beside Pete and said, "Okay, let's get on with it."

I looked at the clock and then at the boys. They caught the hint and ushered everyone out with about as much finesse as they had ushered them in.

When the last one had gone Barb said, "When exactly did we lose control of the situation?"

"About two minutes before they got here," I said, throwing empty cans of Pepsi and cookie boxes into the garbage.

"I'd like to know just how those boys managed to get twenty-five people to Bingo when at the most we can only get fifteen." She laughed. "I'd give a week's wages to have heard their sales pitch."

"It's probably just as well that we didn't!"

The office was cleaned up and we were just about to turn the lights out when the sound of footsteps made us stop. Barbara and I looked at each other and then there she was—"THE MOUTH"!

"Okay, who took my perfume? Somebody here took my perfume!" She was ranting so badly that I was actually afraid she'd swallow her gum.

"Ma'am, you've got it," Barbara said impatiently.

" 'Ma'am, you've got it,' " she mimicked. "If I had it, I wouldn't be here now, would I?" she spat.

Graham and Pete were standing behind her now. She turned on them.

"You took my perfume! Admit it. I know you did!" She was wild with rage and beginning to act a little "schitzie."

"Admit it!" she screamed, stamping her foot on the ground so hard that her glasses fell off the end of her nose. The boys just smiled and, keeping their cool, told her that she must have misplaced it. She finally left and they came in and sat down, satisfaction written all over their faces.

"You clowns did take it, didn't you?" I asked.

"You better believe it," Graham said. "She was such an obnoxious old witch that we gave it to Mr. Mahoney for his wife. She's really sweet and deserves it more than that bag of wind."

"Besides"—Pete laughed—"I can't imagine any trick she could use to turn her husband on. Not even Chanel is that good!"

While the three of them were talking I took the opportunity to sneak next door to go to the john, hoping against hope that it hadn't been torn down, too. I opened the door slowly and peeped in. I felt for the light switch. It was gone. For that matter, so was the wall. I crept in a few more feet, feeling for something—anything. There was nothing. If my need hadn't been so great I would have bolted right out of there, but under the circumstances I had little choice but to continue. I walked slowly, one foot in front of the other, reaching out for support, but found only space. About the only thing they *did* leave was the floor, I thought. My foot hit something.

"Thank God," I sighed, bending down to make sure. I did what I had to as quickly as possible. Mental images of those construction workers in their hard hats with noses pushed up against the windows in our office kept flashing in my mind. They intimidated me enough in the daytime, but here, alone in my indoor outhouse, I was becoming positively paranoid that some of them might be working overtime. I was almost back at the door when I heard breathing.

"Just your imagination," I thought. But my heart began to pound. Suddenly there was a hand on my neck. I screamed. Nothing came out. I screamed again. Not a sound. Running the few feet back to the toilet, I started to flush it furiously. "Noise," I remembered. . . . "Always make a lot of noise!" My voice returned—weak, but better than nothing.

There was familiar laughter. "You can stop flushing the toilet," Graham said. "It's only Barb and I."

"Barb, you're going to pay for this." My threat, as usual, made no impression.

"Don't worry," she said, "I didn't let him in until you flushed the toilet—the first time."

I stood there trying to steady my trembling knees.

"Graham, you'll get me committed yet. Are you going home soon?" I asked.

"Nope."

"Pity!"

When we got back to the office, Pete was busy at one of the work tables finishing a ceramic piece for one of his sisters.

"Is it okay if I stay here for a while to finish this up?" he asked.

"Sure," Barb said. "We're going home now, though, so close up when you're through."

Graham sat down next to Pete. "I think I'll stay, too. I'm not ready to go back up yet."

I asked them if the nurses knew where they were. When they told us that they did, we left a note clearing them with Security, locked the storeroom, and left.

Graham remained in the hospital for nearly a month after that and he and Pete became inseparable. They were both on chemotherapy, and so far they had been able to escape their usual bouts of nausea. They spent more time out on pass than in the hospital. At night they'd visit the local bars, go to the movies, or just walk around the city until the small hours of the morning. They both seemed to be doing well and Pete was benefiting tremendously from Graham's friendship. He no longer was alone, and he knew it.

The night before they were to be discharged was our St. Patrick's Day party and they decided to stick around and "check it out." The weather had been bad that day, with snow, ice, and high winds. Because of this, half of the entertainment had been unable to get there; and the half that did show up were all bombed out of their minds. It made for quite a sight: old men with red bulbous noses and knobby knees that jutted out from beneath their kilts, and carrying bagpipes that none of them were sober enough to play. It was disasater! Michele sat down beside us in a state of total mortification.

"Do you believe this?" she asked. I thought for a minute there she was going to be ill. No words could possibly describe the scene in front of us.

At this point a man from the audience, Mr. O'Malley, jumped up on stage to lend his talents. He had a rich baritone voice and sang beautifully. Maybe something could be salvaged of this party yet, I thought. We began to relax.

"Now, ladies and gentlemen," he announced, taking the mike in his hand, "I'd like to sing my favorite Irish ballad for you."

He began to mingle among the people, and in very soft, melodic tones sang "Danny Boy." We all looked at each other, and then over at Michele, who was bending over with her head in her hands groaning, "Oh no!"

Under the best of circumstances this song brought tears to people's eyes—but here in the hospital we found that more often than not it really upset the patients. So it had become a rule that entertainers were never to sing it. Unfortunately nobody had had a chance to tell Mr. O'Malley this before he'd volunteered to take over. As "Danny Boy" ended, the hush was almost unbearable, and, sensing the change in mood, he quickly said, "Now how about a little Irish joke?"

Graham leaned over and whispered in my ear, "I didn't know he knew you."

I turned in my chair. "You *are* going home tomorrow, aren't you?"

"Yep."

"That's good."

"But I'm coming back." He smiled.

"That's bad!"

Chapter
Five

He was being given a two-week reprieve from the drugs and decided to get as far away from New York as he could. He and a friend went down to Florida to visit his grandmother. He had mixed feelings about this—something to do with a gap of two generations, I think—but he felt confident that he'd get her straightened out in no time. Having known him for seven months, I had no reason to doubt it! I received letters from him saying that they were having a fabulous time, swimming, playing football, and just enjoying the beach and sunshine. He was free, I thought, for the first time in months. For a few blissful weeks he was able to put Memorial out of his mind: the surgery, cobalt, drugs, and all the rest that had claimed precious time from his life.

When he returned he was deeply tanned, he'd regained the weight he'd lost, and he looked the epitome of health. Only he wasn't. He was now coming to clinic for heavy doses of chemotherapy in a further attempt to shrink the remaining tumors in his lungs. He became hyperactive; there was no sitting still. He was like that with us, but he was even worse at home. There, during the day, with his father at work and his brother and friends at school, he had only his mother to keep him company. At first things were all right. They'd talk, drawing closer. But this was only a temporary calm. He began to feel isolated. There was too much time to think about his disease and all of this frustration erupted one afternoon in a huge fight with his mother. It wasn't the first, and it wouldn't be the last, but it was one of the worst. He hurled accusations and insults at her and finally stormed out of the house, leaving her alone to absorb this latest angry exchange between them. She, more than anyone else, bore the brunt of his moods and was the first to admit that she wasn't a strong woman emotionally. She told me once that trying to cope with a son who had cancer while raising Todd, her twelve-year-old, was sometimes more than she could bear.

For a while after that, Graham made it a point to stay away from the house, spending most of his time teaching the kids sports down at the local school. The coach, who had a very special feeling for Graham, was always glad to see him, knowing that he could be of tremendous help to the younger boys, who adored him. The physical activity helped him get rid of his aggression, and he began taking odd jobs, doing everything from chopping wood to washing dishes at a nearby nursing home. He seemed happier and more peaceful than he had for a long time, and a truce was now called between mother and son. The house was constantly filled with his friends in the afternoons, evenings, and weekends and life was beginning to settle into a normal routine again. But this, too, came to a sudden halt when severe and excruciating headaches forced another admission into the hospital.

Chapter
Six

"Mar," Phyllis said, "it's Mrs. Banks for you." She handed me the phone.

"Yes, Mrs. Banks?"

"Mari, Graham's been readmitted and would like to see you. He's in room 439."

I hung up. Another admission, I thought. He's not responding to the drugs as well as he should be. A few years before, a friend of mine had the same type of cancer, and after a year and a half of therapy he was cured. Why was one so lucky and the other suffering so?

Barbara came and stood beside me. "What's the matter?" she asked.

"Graham's back in," I said, resting my head against the wall. "It's such an unfair disease, Barb. A sneaky, stinking disease."

"I know," she said, walking away. "What more can I say?"

I stood up. "Nothing."

When I arrived on the fourth floor Mrs. Banks

was standing in the doorway to his room. She looked tired.

"Do they know yet what's been causing the headaches?" I asked.

She shook her head and pointed toward the room. I looked in. His bed was on the far right and surrounded by interns and residents. We stood talking about nothing in particular, idle chatter mostly. Anything to make the time pass. My God, I thought, they've been in there forever.

Mrs. Banks was becoming increasingly nervous. "He shouldn't have to answer all their questions," she said. "He'll be too tired and wrung out to cope with his own doctors when they get here."

I didn't have an answer for her. Graham must have his reasons. I'd never known him to put up with something that he didn't think was necessary.

Forty-five minutes passed before we were able to see him. He was lying there with his eyes closed, obviously in pain. He opened his eyes and smiled.

"Looks like you're stuck with me again."

"So I see. It's worse this time, isn't it?"

He closed his eyes again. "Yeah, Mar."

Mrs. Banks came and stood behind me.

"Graham," she said, "why did you spend so much time with them? You didn't have to, you know."

He looked up at her and searched her face.

"Mom, maybe what I told them will help some-one else. I've got to try and at least do that."

They just looked at each other and said noth-ing, and I realized then that the gulf between them was widening. Graham had begun to accept what was happening to him, but his mother found it impossible.

Mrs. Banks broke the silence. "Graham," she asked softly, "what do you want from me?"

His eyes glistened, and his voice held a warmth that I'd never heard before. "Your love . . . your support." He paused. "Your understanding, Mom."

He was forcing her to face what she couldn't. He waited for her answer. She didn't have one, and he watched as she turned and left the room.

Graham lay there. "It's tough for her, but someday she'll understand."

I sat down, thinking to myself how little help I was able to give. He winced, covering his eyes with his hand. "Please close my curtain—the overhead light is bothering me." I pulled it around his bed and started to leave.

"Please stay," he said so quietly that I could scarcely hear him. "It hurts to talk, but I don't want you to go." He took my hand and I sat there with him until he fell asleep.

After I left I went looking for Mrs. Banks and found her sitting in the visitors' lounge smoking a cigarette.

"Are you all right?" I asked.

"I don't know any more. Sometimes I feel like my world is being blown to pieces, and there isn't anything I can do to stop it."

In her hands she twisted a flower that she had picked from a nearby bouquet.

"Can we go somewhere and talk?" she asked.

"There's the ninth-floor patio," I answered. "I think we can both use the fresh air."

She nodded and snuffed out her cigarette.

It was one of those rare spring days in New York when the city actually seemed beautiful. We sat for a few minutes letting the warmth of the sun surround us and enjoying the serenity that we found there. Mrs. Banks looked up at the sky.

"Why can't I reach him?" she sighed. "I try so hard. People tell me that I should try to match his courage, but I can't do it. Somewhere he's finding the faith to accept his illness. And what do I do? I discourage him, I tell him to keep on fighting no matter what." She started to cry. "Am I wrong? I don't know what to do any more." Looking at me, she asked, "Why can't I help my own son?"

I thought back to what Graham had said earlier: "Someday she'll understand."

Maybe here, now, I could tell her how he felt. We were close and had talked often, so I knew I could be open with her.

"Mrs. Banks, it's easy for me to sit here and tell you what I think is right, but the hard part is up to you. You have to go through this with Graham step by step. Please don't pull away from him emotionally. He can feel it and he worries about you. It's so important at this time that he should feel your strength and know that he can share with you what's in his heart. He must believe that you've found faith just as he has."

She was picking at the petals of the flower. "Please go on."

Leaning over, I put my hand on her arm. "I can't pretend to know how you feel, but I've seen how love and faith and togetherness have worked miracles. Maybe not physical ones, but emotional ones, and I'm sure that when the time comes you'll match Graham's courage. When he needs you most you'll be there for him. Just as they come to accept in time, so do we." I paused. "That doesn't mean that we ever give up hoping. We just have to trust God, and Graham. It's almost as though he's reached another dimension of life that's difficult for us to comprehend, but we can't be afraid to share it with him.

"You know," I continued, "Kit told us once that it was as though God had a special purpose for these kids and allows them to go through this in order to teach the rest of us about what really matters in this life. I have to believe that, Mrs. Banks, and I want to learn from them."

Phyllis found us then and sat on the wall in front of us.

"I wish my husband were here now," Mrs. Banks went on. "He blames himself for Graham's cancer. He feels that if he hadn't pushed sports with him so much Graham might never have been injured and none of this would have happened."

"We can't live like that," Phyllis said. "It's no good to say 'what if, or if only'—that kind of thinking can eat you up inside. The fact is that it did happen. Graham loves sports, they're a part of him, and whether the injury that he incurred was a direct cause of his cancer is beside the point now. We can't lock ourselves up, or those that we love, for fear of something happening. All they're asking is to live. Not to be afraid of life, but to go out and be involved. We can't take that away from them."

Mrs. Banks looked at us. "You're right," she said, "we can't change the past, we can only hope for the future." She paused. "I just don't know if I can let go of him."

"Sometimes," Phyll said gently, "letting go is the greatest act of love."

Mrs. Banks was still picking at the flower and withdrawing into her own world—a mother's world, one that we didn't belong to. Phyllis got down from the wall and we started to leave.

"Mari," Mrs. Banks said, touching my hand, "will I know when the time comes to let go?"

"Yes," I said, "You'll know."

Graham's headaches persisted for quite a while and most of our visits were spent quietly: no long talks, no laughing, and no pranks. He knew that we were there if he needed anything and at the moment that was all we could do.

Nine days went by and he began to improve. His friends were now beginning to show themselves again, wreaking their usual havoc with the hospital routine. Bubble gum and water bombs began to emerge from the fourth-floor windows, hitting the poor unsuspecting pedestrians below. Unofficial tours of the complex were conducted, with Graham acting as guide to all the areas that were off limits to both patients and visitors, and it wasn't unusual to see a blue-jeaned mob being led by a blond in his bathrobe jogging around the block. They got away with murder, but given a choice we'd take Graham like this any day. His spirits were high now, and one afternoon while we were distributing the schedules he told me that his mother was back in his good graces again. He even admitted that he liked having her around as long as she wasn't "constantly under foot."

I commented half kiddingly and half seriously that it was definitely easier being his friend than his parent. He walked me to the stair well leading to the second floor.

"I know." He laughed. "Count your blessings."

"I do," I called over my shoulder, "believe me, I do!"

I went back down to the office then to finish preparing for the evening's activities. For once in our lives Phyllis and I had gotten our program off smoothly and had the choice of visiting on the floors or relaxing for a while. It was no contest. We opted for the relaxation and took all the necessary precautions to look busy just in case Mr. Lawrence, one of our administrators, came by and nailed us for slacking off. He was young, a regular Brooks Brothers mannequin who never smiled and whose personality was so well hidden that we doubted he even had one. We could never quite figure out exactly what his function was, but when it came to catching us off our guard he was terrific—a regular clairvoyant. So with this in mind we decided to keep a few steps in front of him by taking down bolts of material that were stored on top of the cabinets and spreading them all over the place to look as if we'd been working for hours. Getting at this stuff without breaking your neck was a real trick, and I was beginning to wonder if this character was really worth the trouble. It was at the most critical point, when I was on top of a stool, balancing ever so carefully on two phone books, that Graham came running in.

"Just thought I'd warn you that 'Zelda Zooms' is right behind—" But a shriek from the door interrupted him and made me temporarily lose my footing.

"Oh!" she bellowed. "You're giving me a heart attack up there! Honestly, you should be more careful!"

I didn't have to turn around to know that "Zooms" had indeed arrived. Her real name was Betty Braun. Because of her rather overwhelming appearance she had become the talk of the hospital and acquired a few nicknames during the week she'd been a patient. She wore too much make-up, which prompted Pete to comment that it looked as if the Avon Lady had just blown up on her face, and Graham, never having seen so much mother nature on one body, compared her to a "Sherman tank with a pair of unbelievable headlights." Immediately upon her admission she had appointed herself the hospital's social director, and, above all, she had become infamous for her impromptu singing recitals. So now here she was in all her glory barreling straight for us. Always a great one for theatrics, she thrust her hand in front of her face, announcing that she was about to have a coronary. I dared to sneak a quick look at Graham and Phyllis, who were behind me laughing, when Zelda, seeing that I was still balancing somewhat precariously on the stool, told me firmly to get down. Man, you didn't mess with Zelda, so I did as I was told. No sooner had my feet reached solid ground than she started her act again.

"My God, my heart's beating a mile a minute," she said, "and it's all your fault!" As if to confirm her diagnosis she placed her hand over her chest and, looking me straight in the eye, ordered me to "feel it!"

"How come you get all the breaks?" Graham asked, disappointed that he hadn't been given the job. "Go ahead," he urged and, moving closer, threatened, "If you don't, I will!"

I shot him a look and before I knew what had happened she grabbed my hand and placed it on her huge breast. This is incredible, I thought.

"Can you feel it?" she asked anxiously.

"What?" I said without thinking.

"My heart," she muttered, with an exasperated sigh. Now *that* I felt, but that was about it.

"Well?" she asked, obviously irritated. To be honest, I couldn't feel a thing. Not her heart, anyway, and this whole escapade was getting a little embarrassing, not to mention nerve-racking. So I said, "Frankly, Betty, I don't feel a thing." As soon as the words were out I regretted them. Big dummy, I thought. I should have just agreed with her that the ol' ticker was in trouble and let it go at that. Had it ever dawned on me that she wouldn't let the matter drop I would have lied through my teeth. But that possibility hadn't crossed my mind. All of us were totally unprepared for her next move. She looked from one of us to the other and then proceeded to pick up her breast and heave it over her shoulder.

Graham was incredulous. "I didn't think that was possible," he whispered.

"It's not, for most of us," I assured him.

Zelda, having missed this latest exchange, said, "There now, maybe that's better."

We'd always been told to do anything and everything to make the patients happy, within reason of course. But this was definitely going above and beyond the call of duty. Her breast looked like a knapsack on her back, and, seeing this, I quickly confirmed her findings before Graham offered his assistance again, and begged her to put her anatomy—all of it—back in its proper place. She did so promptly, thank God, and then told us what had brought her down to the office to begin with. She was being discharged the next day, she said, and wanted to repay us for our "many kindnesses" by giving us a "treat." This seemed fair enough, considering tonight's ordeal, and I thought, she's right, she does owe us.

"I'm going to sing 'Climb Ev'ry Mountain' for you," she announced.

"Oh no!" Phyllis moaned. "We don't deserve this."

Zelda waited while we settled into three chairs at the far end of the room. As her lungs filled for the first note Graham just shook his head.

"Man, have those hills grown since Julie Andrews sang it."

At the end of the most piercing rendition of the song we'd ever been subjected to she brushed past us and turned at the door to give one final bow before making her exit. Too stunned to say much, we just sat there and waited for the ringing in our ears to stop.

"What's going on in here?" I looked up, and standing in the doorway was Mr. Lawrence. "I was in the Outpatient Building and heard a terrible racket coming from this office."

Graham walked over and patted him on the back. "You should've gotten here sooner," he said. "You just missed the eighth and ninth wonders of the world!"

Graham left the hospital a few days later, confident that the summer that lay ahead would be the most perfect ever, and it was—at least for a while. The kids spent their days at the Old Mill, the local recreational center where Graham had been a lifeguard the year before. It offered all types of sports and all the beer you could drink for a dollar. At night there were parties, long drives to neighboring New Jersey towns in cars "borrowed" from their unsuspecting parents, and camping trips up to the mountains. The months went by swiftly. Graham's friends had stuck by him for so long and admitted his disease hurt them "like hell inside"—yet they treated him as they always had. Then at the end of August it happened. One of them made an inadvertent slip of the tongue: "I don't want to roughhouse, Graham, you're sick."

It was too much for him. He went home with the words echoing in his head. "You're sick . . . you're sick . . . you're sick . . . !" He stayed only long enough to inform his mother that he was hitching his way up to Cape Cod

"Mom," he said, "it's just something that I have to do. Maybe I have to prove to myself that this thing hasn't gotten the better of me, that I'm still strong and healthy."

His mother was dumfounded. He left. Frightened, she immediately drove up to the Old Mill hoping he would show up in their midst and say that it was all a joke and tell her just to go home and relax. But it wasn't a joke and, scared, they began to search for him. One of the boys climbed to the top of a nearby hill and, shielding his eyes from the afternoon sun, looked down on the highway below. He saw Graham doing exactly what he had set out to do: hitch his way to the Cape —alone.

The Cape held memories of past summers when he had worked cutting trees to earn extra money, where he went sailing and horseback riding, drove for hours along the back roads, and sat on the beaches watching the sun rise and set over the waters. These feelings of peace and contentment awaited him there and he knew it.

"What else could we do but let him go?" his mother said. "He was doing what he felt was right, and that's all that was important."

Graham knew best what he needed, and when he returned he simply said, "They were the five best days of my life. . . . I'm all right now."

Toward the end of September he was involved in a freak automobile accident. The kids were at a party and most of them had had quite a bit to drink. They were outside leaning against a car getting some air when someone in another car backed into them, injuring two boys, one of whom was Graham. When his mother arrived he begged her not to report the accident. No one was that badly hurt and none of them wanted to explain to the authorities the circumstances under which it had all taken place. Mrs. Banks had a typical mother's reaction, but after gentle persuasion and a lot of promises, she agreed. By the next day Graham was complaining of a bad pain in his side, and on September 24 he was readmitted to the hospital.

Barbara and I were down in the admitting office collecting the day's slips when we saw Graham and his mother enter the lobby. He looked well; the summer had obviously agreed with him. But there was one difference. Today, for the first time in a year, his mother was carrying his suitcase. Something stirred in me, but what was it that made me flinch? Why did such a small and insignificant change scare me?

Chapter
Seven

At first we all thought that this admission would be like the others, but it wasn't. He was experiencing more and more pain, running high fevers, and becoming visibly weaker. He spent most of his time down in the X-ray Department or undergoing tests to determine the reason for his sudden turn for the worse.

Mrs. Banks, Phyllis, and I were sitting with him one night and his spirits seemed to be fairly good despite the events of the past few days. He had been talking, but quite suddenly fell asleep in mid-sentence, and because it was late Mrs. Banks decided to go home. She whispered "good night" to him and gently touched his foot as she was leaving. He woke up with a start and screamed, "Why did you do that? . . . You're so stupid—don't you know how much pain I'm in? . . . You scared me!" He was the angriest I'd ever seen him. His eyes were full of fright and burning with indignation.

"Get out—all of you!" he ordered.

I was really shocked, but I wasn't about to stick around to find out what had prompted the outburst. His mother was devastated. We walked to the elevator and stood there in silence.

"I've done it again, haven't I?" she said. "I should have been more careful."

I tried to reassure her that what had happened wasn't her fault. "Don't worry about it, Mrs. Banks. He's been through so much since he's been back in the hospital. Give him time, he'll be okay."

But she seemed to be more concerned about the way he had included us in this latest attack. She asked me to go back and stay with him.

"You're so close," she said. "I'm sure he didn't mean to toss you out too. He needs you. And please tell him I'm sorry."

I was reluctant, but she was insistent and I thought, maybe she's right, maybe he does want to talk. I was wrong. When I returned he was wide awake. He took one look at me and said, "Get out of here, Mar, I told you I want to be left alone!" He made his point, and I left. No encouraging words, no "That's okay, Graham, I understand"—nothing. I was furious. I kept thinking, listen, Graham, I'm not your mother, don't shut me out too. But later I had to admit I wasn't bothered so much that he included me when he got so angry as I was that when I returned he couldn't and wouldn't talk. I was hurt because for the first time I hadn't been able to reach him, and I swore then and there that I'd never go near him again. The next morning, however, I decided to take my chances and went up to his room. When I walked in he was watching television, and it was obvious that he had calmed down considerably from the night before.

"Hey, listen, I'm sorry about yelling at you like that. . . . I don't know what's gotten into me lately. I guess I'm just tired of being sick." He was silent while he tried to find the right words. "I wanted you to stay when you came back last night, but I was so down that I figured it was better to be left alone. Were you mad?"

"Yeah, a little. We just didn't understand, that's all."

There was more to it, though, than he was telling me. I knew him well enough to know when he was holding back. I wanted to ask but, to be perfectly honest, I was a little hesitant— nervous that he'd fly off the handle again if I pursued it.

"Mar," he said in a whisper, "you see Jack over there. Well, he's given up. . . . He shouldn't do that, you know; it frightens me."

Now it was all beginning to make sense. This man who had been a friend of his for so long was dying, and Graham couldn't cope with this—not now, anyway.

I tried as best I could to explain. "Jack hasn't given up, Graham. His body's tired, not his spirit. A time comes, I guess, when you say to yourself, I've given it everything I have, and now it's time to rest."

"It's so hard to watch, though," he sighed; "so hard to understand."

Graham was right, and I knew that nothing I could say would make it any easier for him. This was something he would have to come to terms with on his own. He lay there looking at Jack. Except for a low sound coming from his T.V. the room was so quiet that I began to feel uncomfortable and decided to leave. I'd only gone a few feet when a strange and sarcastic laugh made me turn around. It was Graham. His hand was resting on top of the television, his face was flushed.

" 'The heartbreak of psoriasis,' " he snapped. "What a joke!" He turned the set off and, looking up at me, said softly, "They ought to try the heartbreak of cancer."

He became increasingly agitated during the next few days. The pain was intense and it was then that the doctors decided to move him down the hall into a private room. This time he didn't object. Because of the construction work all windows for that portion of the floor were blocked off, making the room dark and a bit dismal— at least, that's the way it had always seemed before. For some reason, after he moved in, the room took on a more tranquil atmosphere and Graham himself began to settle down. The treatments started working, and gradually he became happier and more like the boy we all knew. Eventually, he even got to the point of throwing an old raincoat on over his pajamas and sneaking out to a friend's home for a couple of hours. He had the nurses' medication schedule down pat and pulled these capers off without ever getting caught. Of course, he told us this in confidence, and far be it from us to blow the whistle on him. In fact, we had to hand it to him for having the smarts and the gumption not only to do it, but to do it and get away with it. Man, if you ever saw some of those nurses on the late shift, you could appreciate the courage it took.

During this time he met and became friends with a six-year-old boy in Pediatrics named Chris, who was a smaller version of Graham in looks, personality, and general unpredictability. It was hard to believe that fate could do that to us, but it happened. On our way back from Ewing one day Phyll and I saw them sitting together in the X-ray Department engaged in what obviously was a very amusing conversation. We weren't going to interrupt them, but Chris spotted us and yelled, "Hey, you two, come here!"

We went over—as if there was a choice—and Chris said, "Listen, Mar, I checked with Mom last night and she said that you're right. You don't have one. What you told me was the truth —you know what I mean, don't you?"

"Yes," I said, "I know what you mean." Trying to avoid the details, I said, "Phyll, let's go, we have to get back to the office."

She stared at me. "Since when did you start caring about that?"

She was right, I couldn't have cared less, but I knew if we stayed there much longer I was going to be in big trouble.

Sensing that there was more to this than I was telling, she sat down on the edge of Chris's chair. "Okay, now what exactly is it that Mari doesn't have?" she asked.

Phyllis was in one of her annoyingly persistent moods, so I quickly took over the explanation before he could.

"Yesterday," I said, "I was reading 'Cinderella' to this imp, and just when we were getting to the good part—"

"Yeah, when the prince tries to make it with Cinderella," Chris interrupted in a voice loud enough to make four or five people turn and smile.

"Chris, he was not trying to make it with her!" I could feel the color rising in my cheeks.

"How do you know?" he asked. "You said he was trying to get it on."

"The slipper, you little devil—he was trying to get the slipper on, and that's *all!*"

By this time a sizable crowd was listening and I found myself trying to clear Cinderella's good name, not to mention my own. Chris opened his mouth to say something.

"Don't you say one word!" I warned.

He was laughing. He had a real talent for embarrassing me half to death and, knowing this, would say almost anything, at any time, in front of anybody. Pity he was so shy and inhibited.

Phyllis loved to see him tie me in knots like this and said, "I know the story, so let's get back to hearing what it is that Mari doesn't have."

"You don't really want to know," I told her.

"Yeah, she does," Chris shouted.

Until now Graham had been sitting there staring at his feet, and his silence was beginning to get to me. Waiting for him to say something was like waiting for the other shoe to drop.

I took a deep breath. "He asked me to show him my birdie."

Graham looked up, the smile on his face spread, and suddenly the room filled with his laughter.

"Now, that must've been one fantastic trick!"

"It was," I said sarcastically and went on, trying to ignore their side remarks. "I told him repeatedly that I didn't have one, but he didn't believe me, and actually accused me of being a fuddy-duddy about the whole thing. He said that he knew that we all had boobies and just naturally assumed that we all had birdies, too. Anyway, I tried to tell him that God made little boys and little girls different, but he wasn't buying any of it, so I begged him to ask his mother for a suitable explanation. All in all, it was a hell of an afternoon."

Graham stretched his legs out in front of him and put his hands behind his head.

"Beats reading fairy tales," he said.

Chris climbed down off the chair and came over to me. "Mom told me I had to say I was sorry for what I called you yesterday just because you wouldn't show me your birdie."

Leaning against me and giving his famous toothless grin, he said, "I don't really think you're an old turkey!"

It was the end of November now and Graham was confined almost totally to his room. Sure, he'd get up and walk the halls for a little while but he didn't have the strength for much else. His parents were given unlimited passes and spent a tremendous amount of time with him, which was what he needed. The understanding and peace that we had all hoped for between Mrs. Banks and Graham started to develop. It was during this period that he exposed a whole other side of himself to us. We never knew before just how deeply his religious convictions ran until he began to talk to us about God. We used to kid him, though, because he'd read the Bible by day and swap dirty jokes with his father by night. His friends, at Graham's request, no longer came to see him. It was more for their sake than anything else. He didn't feel that it was fair for them to have to see him this sick, and perhaps it was for the best because he really wanted this time to be alone with his parents.

At Thanksgiving he asked me to get a card for him and then dictated the following note:

"Dear Mom and Dad,

In my opinion there have never been two greater parents than you. I may get nasty at times, but that's only because I don't feel well. The important thing always is that we all love each other. Let's have a happy Thanksgiving with whatever arises."

He took the pen from me then and with a shaking hand signed it simply:

"Love,
Graham"

The Christmas holidays were upon us again and, as the year before, we were running around in our jeans and T shirts with ladders, cans of paint, and garlands hanging around our necks —just generally looking like the pits. About the only thing that had improved over last year's appearance was the ol' complexion. We'd learned our lesson. As fast as the chocolate came in, it went out again—to anybody; let them reap the benefits this year. How about that for the Christmas spirit—free zits!

Because our time was limited we visited Graham early in the morning, at lunch, and again fairly late at night after the family had gone. One morning I went up to check on him. He was restless, pushing his breakfast around on the plate, and he stated curtly that "it sucked."

He had a real way with words, short and to the point. He seemed preoccupied, more so than usual, and I thought that maybe he just wanted to be left alone, so I started to leave.

"Wait," he said, putting his fork down. "Have you ever heard of Kathryn Kuhlman?"

"Yes I have. Why?"

"Do you believe in the power of healing?"

"I think God uses His powers of healing through people." And again I asked him why the sudden interest.

"She's going to be at the Americana this weekend and I sort of wanted to go, but the doctors aren't too keen on having me moved." There wasn't much I could say to that. It didn't take a genius to see that Graham was sick and to let him out in this cold weather might be asking for trouble. I sat down beside him and waited for him to continue.

"Maybe it's just as well. . . . All those people there, and I'd have to go in on a stretcher. . . . I'd feel like a freak, a regular side show. . . ." His eyes clouded and he looked away.

"Look at me," he said, "bald, skinny. . . .

100

People would stare, and feel sorry for me. I don't want their damn sympathy! I don't need it!"

The tears rolled down his cheeks. It was the first time I'd ever seen him like this. I wanted to reach out, say something, anything to ease the hurt—sometimes it's better, though, just to sit and listen. But he had said all that he was going to. I placed my hand under his chin and made him face me.

"Do you feel sorry for yourself?" I asked.

"No."

"Then they won't, either." I paused. "Graham, it's how you feel about yourself that's important."

"I know," he said, "but once in a while I forget that."

"Well, remember this, anyone who goes to Kathryn Kuhlman has problems, too, and that puts you all pretty much in the same boat, right?"

He nodded.

"Okay, then, if you saw someone who was sick and in pain being wheeled in on a stretcher, would you think of him as a freak or would you pray along with the others for a healing?"

He looked at me and smiled. "I'd pray for him."

"Okay, there you have it. Try giving people the benefit of the doubt—they're a lot more understanding than you might think."

"Yeah. You know, every once in a while you make a lot of sense."

"About time you realized that."

He laughed. "One more thing, Mar. Could you

sneak me up some food for lunch? I can't stomach any more of this slop!"

I looked at his tray and had to admit that what was on it was no bargain, so I promised to bring him a hamburger, french fries, and a Coke later on that afternoon. I started to go.

"You're all heart," he said, putting his hand on my shoulder.

We'd been through this routine a million times before and he knew damn well that I wasn't going to foot the bill. I turned around to face him. "I hate to disillusion you again, but either you fork up the money or you forfeit the food. On my salary I can't afford to have a heart."

He reached into his drawer and reluctantly pulled out a dollar bill. "Like I said, you're all heart."

It was late afternoon on the following day when we heard it: "Attention please! Attention please! Code 4, Memorial. Code 4, Memorial." Barbara and I stopped cold while the message was repeated: "Attention please. Code 4, Memorial." Something stirred in my gut. I had checked on Graham only an hour or so before—he was fine. This emergency code couldn't possibly be for him. We went back to the office and Phyllis was sitting by the phone.

"The code was for Graham," she said. "They've just put him on critical." Barb and I ran up the stairs to the fourth floor. Mrs. Banks was leaning against the wall visibly shaken but in remarkable control of herself. We went over to her. She told us that Graham was bleeding badly and she asked me to go in. Barbara stayed with her while I got into the isolation gown, mask, and gloves. As I pushed open the door I could hear the doctors relaying orders to Graham's nurse, and the atmosphere was one of quiet urgency. I thought, what the hell am I doing in here? I can't even see Graham, and there isn't a damn thing I can do. Mr. Banks walked over and put his arm around me.

"He'll be all right, he's just got to be," he said. "He's still conscious—let him know you're here."

I didn't know what to say. "Maybe later," I told him, "not now."

I just stood there thinking, this is all some sort of a bad joke. It's strange, but at a time like that your mind goes blank. You're there physically, but somehow you feel as if you're completely detached from the whole scene. You want to push a button and see what's on the other channels, only it's not that simple. I kept wondering what Graham was thinking, feeling—was he frightened? Dear God, please don't let him be afraid. Mr. Banks's grip tightened around my shoulder. It was as though he were reading my mind. He kept repeating in barely audible whispers, "He'll be all right."

They took Graham up to surgery and we stayed with the family. We talked, drank coffee, and prayed for what seemed like an eternity and then, finally, he was brought back to his room. They gave him something to make him sleep and, for a while at least, the tension subsided. Early the next morning he started hemorrhaging badly again and everyone thought he couldn't possibly make it through the day. The whole thing was worse than the day before, it all seemed so unreal. It just wasn't happening, not to Graham. My heart and my mind just wouldn't accept it.

People said, "He's going to die." The nurses were crying and the doctors were upset. Terrifying as it all seemed, I just knew that he was going to make it. Our supervisor was understanding and let us forget about the decorating for that day, so we stayed with him on the fourth floor.

Three days . . . a week . . . ten days passed and he began to stabilize. He was conscious during this time and we could all see a change taking place. He became very concerned about his family. Graham knew what his disease was doing to his parents and his brother. He worried about them. Was his mother getting enough rest? Was his father missing too much work? Could their marriage survive the emotional torment that his cancer was unloading on them? He had said often, "I worry that if something happens to me, Mom and Dad will get a divorce." I asked him if he'd talked to his parents about this.

"Yeah, my mom. She said that if they've put up with each other for this long, then they can put up with each other forever." He paused, and you could sense his overwhelming relief.

"She was smiling, Mar, when she told me that. . . . I believe her. . . . I couldn't stand it if they broke up because of me."

And then there was Todd, his brother, who was being left at home alone and was going through his own private hell. There was a time in the past when the brothers didn't get along at all, and their differences were great. Todd felt that he had to compete with his older brother. To him Graham was the tall, good-looking boy who excelled in sports, who was immensely popular, and who now, because of this disease, was depriving him of a family life. He was terribly confused and hurt and would lash out at Graham without meaning to. He'd received a motor bike and refused to let Graham near it, saying, "It belongs strictly to me!" But as Graham became sicker the boys drew closer and were more understanding of one another. Todd even wrote a note to Graham in the hospital:

"This is the key to the bike. It's all yours, so don't lose it. The bike is here waiting for you."

Those few words meant the world to Graham. "I feel so sorry for Todd," he said; "he's had to suffer with this too."

His family was uppermost in his mind. He wanted to make sure that they were going to be all right. In his own way he was preparing them. Each day his faith became stronger and his belief touched all of us who knew him. Whenever he spoke to us he'd say, "I'm okay now, I'm going to be fine . . ." and you believed him.

The doctors had done all that was possible for him now and the one thing that Graham wanted most was to go home for Christmas. That morning he asked me to come and see him the night before he was to be discharged.

"I want to talk," he told me, "but I don't want my parents, or anybody for that matter, to hear what I have to say. I'm going to ask Mom and Dad to leave early."

He wouldn't tell me what this was all about and asking questions wasn't going to get me anywhere, so I left. There was something so different about him now, but if you had asked me what it was I wouldn't have been able to put it into words. He'd look at you with such an intensity that it was as though he could see straight into your heart; and there was always a flicker of a smile that crossed his face as though he was guarding some secret that no one else knew about. I'd never said anything to him about it, but today it had been particularly disarming and I didn't know why. I went through the motions of wrapping packages and tending to the last-minute details that inevitably came up before the holidays—but the day went slowly and my thoughts constantly went back to that look in his eyes this morning. What was it that he wasn't telling anyone?

It was five to seven when I stepped off the elevator and the floor was unusually quiet for that time of the evening. Except for Mr. and Mrs. Banks, there was no one else in the hall. They were standing outside of Graham's room.

"He's asked us to leave," Mrs. Banks said. "He said that there was something important that he had to talk to you about. Do you know what it is?"

I felt uneasy. I loved them, and I didn't want them to feel as if I was keeping anything from them.

"I'm sorry," I said, "I really don't have any idea what's on his mind. He wouldn't tell me this morning, either."

They were warm and understanding people and I could tell they knew that sometimes it was easier for two people close in age to communicate, so they didn't press the issue. They kissed me good-night and I went in.

"Okay, Banks, this better be good!"

He smiled. "It's important, Mar. I'm sorry I had to ask Mom and Dad to leave, but I'm not sure they're ready to hear what I have to say."

I stood there, not moving. "And I am?"

"Yes."

The room was dark with the exception of one little light over in the corner, and as I moved the chair over by his bed I could feel him watching me. The bed was slightly elevated so that I

107

had to look up. Graham shifted position so that his face rested against the bars.

"There's no more time left, you know, and I need answers. . . . I'm not afraid. . . . I guess I just want to know that there's been a reason for all this."

He went on: "Have you ever wondered why God lets some of us go through hell and lets others of us lead carefree lives without any problems at all?"

"I've thought about it a lot, Graham, but there are no clear-cut answers—at least, none that I know of. We're all here for different reasons, each of us with something special to give. It's up to each person to determine the meaning of his life. We can only try to do the best with what we're given."

"Do you really believe that we're here for a reason? That maybe all of this I've gone through means something? Damn it, I'm sixteen years old and what have I done? Sometimes I think that I've got to do or say something that will make this all worth it. I'm dying, Mar, and I know it."

I wasn't prepared for this to be the topic of our conversation, and it scared me. I thought, I'm not equipped to handle this situation. Suppose I say the wrong things. A chaplain, a doctor, someone like that should be here. They'd know what to do. I leaned my head against the back of the chair and closed my eyes. God help me, I thought.

"Mar?"

I opened my eyes and his hand stretched out through the bars toward me. I took it and held on tight.

"You're my friend," he said. "You have been through this whole mess. I just want someone to talk to, okay? I know you don't have all the answers, but you said you've thought about it—what do you feel? Please tell me."

The atmosphere changed then. I wasn't being asked to supply the impossible—just to share myself with him, that was all.

"Someone I loved very much once told me that life was a series of one person touching another —learning and giving to others what we've been taught. Love has a certain responsibility and so does care. If we keep it to ourselves and refuse to share it, then those experiences don't amount to much; but if we pass it along, then everything that we stand for as people goes on long after we do. Graham, if it hadn't been for this person I wouldn't even be working here. You and I never would have met and we wouldn't be having this talk now. It's kind of like a chain reaction, and once it's started it doesn't stop. What's real in a person can never be destroyed by anything."

He put his head back on the pillow and let go of my hand. "This person died, didn't he?"

"Yes, he did."

". . . And you still love him, don't you?"

"Yes, I do, very much."

"Why?"

Graham was asking me to tell him something I'd never shared with anyone. Not because I didn't want to, but because I couldn't. All these years and those words that had guided my life still remained just between myself and a boy not much older than Graham—my brother. Maybe it was selfish on my part. I don't know. But if what I'd said earlier was to have any truth, then the time had come for me to open up. Never was it as important as now, and I knew it.

"I guess because he told me that we could never be separated again physically," I said; "that now if I ever needed him, all I had to do was think of him and he'd be right there with me. He's never broken that promise. It's strange, but in some ways I feel closer to him now than I did before. He's with me every step of the way —very much alive in my heart."

That intense look was back on Graham's face. "He's always with you . . . kind of like keeping you on the straight and narrow, eh?" He smiled. "He's got a full-time job." He paused. "So that's love. . . . It lives on through the people that we leave behind."

He lay there and said nothing for a few minutes.

"I know now what I have to do. There's some paper and a pencil in the top drawer. I want you to write a letter to my cousin Brian for me, okay?

110

He's been getting really screwed up on drugs and having a rough time of it. If I can reach him . . . if I can help, then all of this will have made sense."

He turned on his side and started to dictate.

"Dear 'Short hair':

Well, how the hell are you? You're right, it's pretty damn boring lying in this hospital bed. After eleven weeks it gets pretty damn sickening. Yeah, looking at the same damn walls day in and day out. When I first came in I thought it was going to be a breeze, in and out real slick—but then everything got all screwed up. I had tubes in my arms and one big mother down my nose. After that (whether you know it or not this is only the second week) then I really started getting a lot of pain. You know, like something or someone was beating me with a bat in my chest—and these damn doctors started running me through all these tests and you know, Bri, all these damn doctors, it was a big waste—they were completely wrong. So one day I was in a room with four people and I'm gonna be moved to a single room (and oh by the way, this is all past B.S. I'm giving you, because this is all leading up to the four best days of my life).

Yeah, I started taking the pain medication through my rear, and it wasn't half bad because I got a great high out of it—at least for a while—oh by the way, I don't know about the crap they feed you there, but the stuff you get here—wow, it really stinks sometimes. I've lost forty-three pounds—pure skin and bones, and after a week of needles in my tail I was like a pincushion—and then I started taking them in my arms and then they became like wet spaghetti, and my tail now is completely perforated. Now I finally get to move into my own little cottage so to speak. One room, no windows, an air conditioner, and I'm completely tied up in bed and can't get out. So you know what it's like, then. I gotta take a dump in bed, take a leak in bed—that isn't half bad. . . ."

At this point he became aware that I was having trouble keeping up with him.

"Is my language upsetting you?" he asked.

The concern on his face made me laugh. "Your language? No! You're just going a little fast, that's all. I told you that I flunked Speed-writing and I'm having trouble trying to find suitable symbols for some of your words."

"I've got some you could use!"

"Forget it!" I said. "I'd rather use my own."

He laughed. "You still don't trust me."

"Should I?"

"Nope! Okay, now where were we?"
I told him, and he continued.

"So all right, the first day I get my private-
duty nurse and it's 8 A.M. (By the way, Bri,
you wouldn't believe, I've got the coolest
bed, it's all electric.)
. . . And I'm in my room with my nurse
and my electrical bed—well, anyway, what
happened was I had blankets on me and all
of a sudden I smelled this really horrible
stinking odor. Well, Bri, I sprung a leak. It
may sound funny, but it happened on the
same side as my lung operation was on. I
popped a nice hole that started leaking
poison and that's what the smell was. I had
already lost 300 cc.'s before my nurse and
I noticed it. But oh, God what a smell! So
anyway, she had a pan and just started collecting all the poison that was coming out
of my chest. Finally the doctors came in and
bandaged me up and called my lung surgeon. So four o'clock that afternoon I went
to the O.R. All right, get this, I'm on the
operating table and only half drugged.
What they did to me finally was put a tube
inside the hole, which was about the size of
a half dollar. You know, all right, that
wasn't half bad. I returned from surgery
and everything seemed to be okay—it was
pumping the liquid out of my chest like it

113

was supposed to. So now it's about six o'clock, so I said screw it, I was going to sleep for the night. Meanwhile every three hours I was getting pain shots. So you know, I made it through the night, thank God. The next morning was the beginning of what most people thought was the beginning of the end. Well, I woke up, had my breakfast, and it was time to roll over on the side that I had burst. All right, ready, Brian? All right, my nurse told me to roll over on my right side, which was the side with the hole in it —picture me now with this tube—so all right, I rolled over, and my nurse said that everything was all clear—and then after about thirty seconds there was something I've never seen before—myself bleeding to death—yeah, Brian, dying. I didn't know what it was at first. The cover was still on top of me. So I asked my nurse to come over and check it—and Brian, when she pulled off the covers and I rolled over on my back I didn't know what to think. From then on, Brian, I was in such a state of shock that I didn't feel much pain. By now my bed was under about three inches of blood. The doctors and interns are trying to do all they can for me, but they needed a surgeon, and they were all in the operating rooms. So they did their best to stop the bleeding. I don't know if you've ever seen 'Medical

Center' with those poles with the bottles hanging from them. Well, they're called I.V. poles, and mine was full of packs of blood and plasma, and a lot of other stuff. The only thing that saved my life was the fact that I went into an extreme state of shock. Finally the surgeon came and patched me up. I got some dose of medication that knocked me clean off my tail. So I went to sleep, and the next morning I woke up, which was the second miracle because neither the doctors nor my nurse or anybody thought I would make it because of the amount of blood I had lost the day before. So ever since then I've just been trying to get myself back together. I can't really walk yet and I'm weak as hell.

Bri, I've never thought much about dying before, but I am now. There's gotta be something to this business, and I want my life to have had some meaning—maybe just to touch someone. That's why I'm writing all of this crap to you. Maybe just to help, just so that I don't feel that all of this I've gone through is for nothing. Brian, believe me, anything you go through cannot be half as bad. So please do me a favor, even if you get some idiot bugging the hell out of you up there, just remember, Brian, you've got everything going for you. You can walk and use your hands—you have a chance at life—to really live, Brian. Don't screw it! You have everything that I don't any more. You see, I had to have a beautiful girl write this for me.

Love,
Graham"

It was close to eleven o'clock when he finished, and there wasn't anything left to say. He had said it all.

He closed his eyes and sighed, "I hope Brian understands."

I held the letter in my hand and looked around the room. There on his bedside table, lying side by side, were his Bible and the latest issue of *Playboy* magazine. It was too much. They seemed to sum Graham up: "The sinner and the saint," his mother had said. The tears that had been threatening came and there was nothing I could do to stop them. Everything that we had shared that night, everything that he had said in his letter, was all true and now, finally, I had to admit that Graham was going to die. I felt his hand lightly touch my head.

"It's okay," he said.

I looked up at him and nodded. "I know."

He lay back quietly and we were silent. A few minutes later he said, "I've thought of something else, Mar."

I picked up the pencil but he took it from my hand. "That isn't what I meant." A smile crept over his face. "Which one of us is gonna spring for the stamp?"

Early the next morning I met him down in the lobby where he was lying bundled up on a stretcher waiting to be taken home. We had been there for only a few minutes when the men from the ambulance came and moved him outside.

"Look, Mar, it's snowing," he said. "I'm going to have a white Christmas—the best and most beautiful Christmas of my life." He closed his eyes and let the snow fall on his face. I stood there watching him. He was so happy, so content, and so completely at peace with himself.

His parents came over. "It's time to leave," Mr. Banks said softly.

Graham looked up at me. "I don't know how to say good-by to you," he said; "I don't want to."

"I don't want that, either, so we won't, okay? We'll see each other again—someday."

He lifted his arms from beneath the blankets and hugged me. His grip tightened around my neck.

"Remember me," he whispered. "Please remember me."

His arms fell to his sides and I backed away, knowing that the moment had come for me to let go.

Graham's prophecy came true. He was the only

one who knew that this was to be the best and most beautiful Christmas of his life. He died on December 23.

I will remember him always.

ABOUT THE AUTHOR

Mari Brady grew up on the North Shore of Long Island with her parents and three brothers and now lives in Manhattan. While working for an international youth group, she became interested in other countries' cultures and lifestyles and traveled throughout Europe and Africa. Her main concerns are hospital work and medicine, and she met Graham Banks when she was a recreation aide at Memorial Sloan-Kettering Cancer Center in New York City. **Please Remember Me** is her first book.

GROWING UP...
You Can't Run Away
from It and
You Don't Have To!